PIERPONT GENEALOGY

AND CONNECTING LINES,

PARTICULARLY

REV. JOHN PIERPONT

OF HOLLIS STREET CHURCH
BOSTON, MASSACHUSETTS.

COMPILED FROM AUTHENTIC SOURCES
BY HIS GRANDDAUGHTER

MARY PIERPONT BARNUM.

EDITED BY HIS GRANDSON

ARTHUR EDWIN BOARDMAN.

PRINTED BY HIS GREATGRANDSON
JAMES ALLEN CROSBY.
BOSTON, 1928

REV. JOHN PIERPONT
1785—1866.

INTRODUCTION

REV. JOHN PIERPONT (XXV)

The first Pierpont was Sir Hugh de Pierrepont, Lord of Castle Pierrepont in the southern confines of Picardy, six miles from St. Sauveur, Normandy, in 980., whence, the chronicler tells us, the family received the name. Not finding a ferry there, Charlemagne caused a *Stone Bridge* to be built, giving the name *Pierre-ponte* to the place.

A younger son of the family, one Sir Robert Pierrepont, Knight, went from France to England in 1066. as a Commander under William the Conqueror, and was given large estates in Sussex and Suffolk. He was ancestor to Sir Henry Pierrepont, born 1545, who married Frances Cavendish, a direct descendant of William the Conqueror's daughter and the Earls of Surrey and Warwick. Their son, made Earl of Kingston in 1628., had a cousin, James Pierpont, who lived in Derbyshire and carried on trade between England and Ireland. In time the business expanded to the Colonies across the Atlantic and two of James' sons came to America, where one, the Hon. John Pierpont, who married Thankful Stowe, settled for life in 1640., buying, in 1656., three hundred acres of land in Roxbury, Mass. He was born in London, 1619., died December 7, 1682., a man of substance, and sent his eldest son James to Harvard College.

This son became the Rev. James Pierpont, one of the founders of Yale College, and lectured to the students as Professor of Moral Philosophy. He was called to the First Church of New Haven in 1685., at the age of twenty-five years, and was there provided with a stately home by his parishioners. He was father-in-law to Jonathan Edwards, who married his daughter Sarah, and was a great friend of Cotton Mather. In 1698. he, with two other ministers, conceived the idea of founding a college, and in the ensuing year ten of the principal ministers of the Colony were chosen as Trustees of the institution. It was originally established at Saybrooke but was removed to New Haven in 1716., two years after the death of Rev. James Pierpont.

One son of his, James Pierpont, who married Anna Sherman, was a tutor at Yale; and a grandson, James, who married Elizabeth

3

Collins, of South Farms, Litchfield, was the father of Rev. John Pierpont, of Hollis Street Church, Boston, Massachusetts.

Rev. JOHN PIERPONT was born at Litchfield, South Farms, on the 6th. of April, 1785., where the first Law School in the land was founded in 1784. He graduated from Yale College in 1804., in the class with John C. Calhoun. The following year he went to Charlestown, S. C. as tutor in the family of Col. Allston, the son-in-law of Aaron Burr. In 1811. he was admitted to the Bar. In 1810. he was married to his fourth cousin, Mary Sheldon Lord, who traced her ancestry back to King Alfred, of England, along a path thickly strewn with strawberry leaves. They were married by the Rev. Lyman Beecher and lived in Litchfield for a few years. Afterwards he lived at Newburyport, Mass., where, in 1812. he wrote "The Patriot", soon after the mob in Baltimore had destroyed the office of "The Federal Republican" and murdered General Lingan.

Later he moved to Boston and opened a law office on Court Street, and there formed a lasting friendship with John Neal. With his brother-in-law, Joseph Lord, he went into a retail and jobbing dry-goods business on Court and Washington Streets. In 1815. they moved to Baltimore, where they opened a wholesale business with John Neal as an added partner. In little more than a year they failed, through being defrauded by their agents in Charleston. He paid back the last dollar he owed after many years of toil and economy. He then went to the Divinity School in Cambridge, (Harvard), and in 1819. when 34. years old, he accepted a call to Hollis Street Church, Boston. In 1825. he, with other young ministers, formed the American Unitarian Association.

Before 1825. Rev. John Pierpont had been made Chaplain of the State Senate, Trustee of the Boston Public Library and a member of the School Committee. He had also had the degree of Master of Arts conferred upon him by both Yale and Harvard Colleges.

In 1825., when Lafayette laid the corner stone to Bunker Hill Monument, Daniel Webster delivered the oration and John Pierpont wrote for the occasion his "Warren's Address before the Battle of Bunker's Hill" beginning, "Stand! The ground's your own, my braves!"

In 1836. he spent some months in Europe for his health. In October, 1838. he wrote his resignation to the Hollis Street pulpit, but his friends withheld it. Then came the "Seven years war" in

BIRTHPLACE OF REV. JOHN PIERPONT.
LITCHFIELD, SOUTH FARMS,
CONNECTICUT.

the church. At the end the Council exonerated him and the Supreme Court of the churches confirmed the finding of the Council and awarded him $13,000. After that he resigned.

In 1840. he published his only collected volume of verse under the name, "Airs of Palestine and other poems". The "Airs of Palestine" was written in Baltimore, in 1816. After resigning from Hollis Street Church he went to Troy, N. Y., where he preached four years in the First Unitarian Church, returning to New England in 1849. as Pastor of the Unitarian Church at Medford, Mass.

His 80th. birthday was celebrated in Washington, April 6th.-1865. a few days before his friend Abraham Lincoln was assassinated.

Besides his well known activities in the cause of temperance and abolition of slavery, he was largely instrumental in abolishing the law of imprisonment for debt in Massachusetts.

GENEALOGY OF PIERPONT FAMILY

TAKEN FROM "BARTOW"

PIERREPONT vs PIERPONT

I. SIR HUGH DE PIERREPONT, A.D. 980. Lord of Castle Pierrepont in the south confines of Picardy and Diocese of Loare, a branch of the Pierreponts who were lords of Castle Pierrepont, two leagues from St. Sauveur, NORMANDY, from whence they derived their name. The place derives its name from a stone bridge with which Charlemagne supplied the place of a ferry.
His son,

II. SIR GOD-FREY, succeeded him and was father of Godfrey and Robert. Godfrey, son of Sir Godfrey, was father of Sir Ingolbrand, Lord of Castle Pierrepont, Picardy, A.D. 1090, and ancestor of the French Pierreponts. The younger son,

III. SIR ROBERT DE PIERREPONT, Knt., came over from France to England as a commander in the army of the Conqueror, 1066, from whom he received great estates in the counties of Suffolk and Sussex, among which was the Lordship of Hurst Pierrepont. His son was

IV. WILLIAM DE PIERREPONT, 2nd Lord of the Manor of Hurst Pierrepont. His son,

V. SIMON DE PIERREPONT, 3rd of Hurst Pierrepont, was at the siege of Acre, and was succeeded by his son,

VI. WILLIAM, who was succeeded by a younger son,

VII. ROBERT, 6th Lord of the Manor of Hurst Pierrepont and father of

VIII. SIR HENRY, Knt. "A person of great note," fought in the battle of Louves, 1264. Died 1292. He married Annora, only daughter of Sir Michael de Manvers, Lord of Holme Manor, of which he became possessed under the name of Holme Pierrepont, County Nottingham.
(This place is still in the family, the present proprietor

MOTTO
"SPES TUTISSIMA COELIS"

PIERPONT ARMS
"ARGENT. — A SEMEE OF CINQUEFOIL GULES—
A LION RAMPANT, SABLE.
CREST, A FOX."

being Herbert Pierrepont, Earl Manvers, Viscount Newark and Baron Pierrepont, Knt.) Sir Henry's younger son,

IX. SIR ROBERT DE PIERREPONT, Knt., 3d. proprietor of Holme Pierrepont, married Sarah, daughter of Sir John de Heing, Knt., and was succeeded by his son,

X. HENRY DE PIERREPONT, who married Mary, daughter of Sir William Fitswilliams, Knt. They had Henry and a younger son,

XI. SIR EDMUND DE PIERREPONT, maternally descended from the kings of France and England, Counts of Normandy, Flanders and Anjon. He was 6th. proprietor of Holme Pierrepont. He died at Gascoign, France, 1370., having married Joan, daughter of Sir George Montboncher of Gohurlston, Nobbs., and was succeeded by his son,

XII. SIR EDMUND DE P. who married Frances, daughter of Sir Wm. Frank, Knt., by whom he had one son,

XIII. SIR HENRY DE P. He married Helen, daughter of Sir Nicholas Lankford, by whom he had an only son,

XIV. HENRY, who married Thomasine, daughter of Sir John Melton, of Melton Hall, County Derby, by whom he had Henry, who d.s.p. and a younger son,

XV. FRANCIS, 11th. of Holme Pierrepont, who married Margaret, daughter of Mr. John Burden, and had,

XVI. WILLIAM, who married Joan, daughter of Sir Richard Empson, by whom he had,

XVII. SIR GEORGE, only son, 13th. of Holme Pierrepont and lord of several manors in Nottingham and Derby, and one of the Knights of the Carpet, that were made at the Coronation of Edward VI, 1541. He died March, 1564. By his second wife, Winifred, he had five children viz:—

XVIII. SIR HENRY, 14th. of Holme Pierrepont born 1545., married Frances,* daughter of Sir Wm. Cavendish, died March 19,-1615. and buried in St. Edmund's Church,

*See Folio 27

Holme Pierrepont. His son, Sir Robert, was created
Earl of Kingston, in 1628. and was ancestor of Evelyn,
Duke of Kingston, who died without posterity in 1773.
2. Gervase.
3. WILLIAM, married Elizabeth Harris, died 1687.
4. A daughter, married Sir John Harpur.
5. Anne, mother of Francis Beaumont.

XIX. WILLIAM PIERREPONT of Holme Pierrepont, who
married Elizabeth Harris, of Lankashire, had

XX. JAMES, of Holme Pierrepont and cousin to Sir Robert,
Earl of Kingston. He was heir to a large estate in
Derbyshire and carried on a trade between England and
Island; came to America to visit his sons and died at
Ipswich, Mass. By his wife, Margaret, he had five
children, viz:—

XXI. 1. JOHN, born 1619. in London.
2. Robert, born in London, 1621.
3. Mary, born in Ireland.
4. Anne.
5. Martha.

XXI. JOHN PIERPONT, born in London, 1619., married
Thankful Stow. He settled near Boston in 1640. In
1656. he purchased 300. acres of land, now the site of
Roxbury. He was a Magistrate in 1640. and died
December 7,-1682. His elder son,

XXII. JAMES PIERPONT,† born at Roxbury, Mass. January 4.-
1659., graduated at Harvard 1681. and settled in New
Haven, Conn., in 1685. as pastor of the First Congrega-
tional Church. He was one of the founders of Yale
College. Died November 14.-1714. On July 26.-1698.
he married, for his third wife, Mary Hooker, daughter
of Rev. Samuel Hooker of Cambridge, Mass., by whom
he had

XXIII. JAMES PIERPONT, JR., who married Anne Sherman
March 28.-1758., and Rev. Samuel Pierpont*, pastor of
First Church in Lyme, Connecticut, born December 30.-

*See Folio 24   †See Folio 15

REV. JOHN PIERPONT, AT 80 YEARS.

1700., drowned March 15.-1723. when crossing the Connecticut River.

James Pierpont, Jr. (XXIII.) born at New Haven, Conn., May 21.-1699. Married Anne Sherman, March 28.-1758., by whom he had,

XXIV. JAMES PIERPONT, 3d. born January 4.-1761., married, September 24.-1782., Elizabeth Collins, daughter of Charles Collins and Anne Huntingdon, his wife. Elizabeth died July 28.-1815. Their second son,

XXV. JOHN PIERPONT, (Rev.) born April 6.-1785., at Litchfield, Conn., married by Rev. Lyman Beecher, September 23.-1810. to Mary Sheldon Lord, born January 31.-1787., daughter of Lynde Lord, Esq., and Mary Lyman, his wife. She died at Medford, Mass., August 23.-1855. and is buried in Mount Auburn Cemtery, Cambridge, Mass. They had six children.

1. William Alston Pierpont, born at Litchfield, Conn., July 11.-1811. married at Syracuse, N. Y. by Rev. Mr. Wilkins, Maria Cecelia Ridgeway. He died at New York May 4.-1860. and is buried in Greenwood Cemetery, Brooklyn, N. Y.

2. Mary Elizabeth, born in Newburyport, Mass., September 18.-1812., married at Macon, Ga., David Flanders, April,-1865., died at Atlanta, Ga. October 15.-1896. s. p., and is buried in Mount Auburn Cemetery, Cambridge, Mass.

3. Juliet, born at Baltimore, Md., July 30.-1816, married May 2.-1836. Junius Spencer Morgan, a noted banker and financier, of Hartford, Conn., later of London, England. She died February 23.-1884.

4. John Pierpont, Jr., (Rev.) born at Boston, Mass., November 22.-1819. Married first, Joanna Le Barron Sibley, and for his second wife Anne Haven, daughter of Franklin Haven, a prominent banker of Boston. He died April 30.-1879., and is buried in Mount Auburn Cemetery, Cambridge, Mass.

XXVI. 5. James Lord Pierpont, born at Boston, Mass., April 25,-1822. Married in Troy, N. Y., September 4.-1846., Millicent Cowee, daughter of Farwell Cowee and Abagail Merriam, his wife, born in Westminster, Mass.,

June 22.-1822., died at West Medford, Mass., the home
of Rev. John Pierpont, August 17.-1856., and is buried
in Mount Auburn Cemetery, Cambridge, Mass. For his
second wife he married, in Savannah, Ga., Eliza Jane
Purse, and died at Winter Haven, Fla. August-1893. and
is buried in Savannah, Ga.
6. Caroline Augusta, born at Boston, Mass., August 21.-
1823., married September 27,-1848. at Troy, N. Y., to
Joseph M. Boardman of Macon, Ga., who was born at
Newburyport, Mass., May 10.-1808. and died June 28.-
1893. She died at Macon, Ga., September 17.-1881., and
is buried in Rose Hill Cemetery.

The Rev. JOHN PIERPONT, after the death of his first wife, and
mother of his children, was married at Pawling, Duchess Co.,
N. Y., by Rev. Dr. Farley, of Brooklyn, N. Y., to Harriet
Louise, widow of Dr. George W. Fowler, and daughter of
Archibald Campbell, of Campbellville in the town of Pawling.
She was born May 20.-1811. and married to Rev. John Pierpont
December 8.-1857. They had no children. He died at Med-
ford, Mass. August 27.-1866., and was first buried there, but
now lies in Mount Auburn Cemetery, Cambridge, Mass., on
Lavender Path near Mountain and Magnolia Avenues.
The inscription on his monument at Mount Auburn is:

POET

PATRIOT

PREACHER

PHILOSOPHER

PHILANTHROPIST

PIERPONT

HYDE.

ELIZABETH HYDE married Rev. Timothy Collins, first minister of Litchfield, Conn. He was son of John Collins and Anna Teete, granddaughter of Governor William Teete of Guilford. Their son,

CHARLES COLLINS, married Anne Huntingdon. Of their ten children their daughters Elizabeth, Lois and Rhoda married

PIERPONTS.

Elizabeth married James,

Lois married Robert,

Rhoda married Evelyn.

Mrs. Frances Pierpont Laselle is authority for the following:— There was to be a double wedding of the oldest pair of lovers and the youngest. Just two weeks before this double ceremony took place, they exchanged partners. The oldest Pierpont brother took the youngest Collins sister and vice versa. Rev. John Pierpont was son of the eldest brother and was fifteen years older than Mrs. Laselle, who was the daughter of Evelyn, the youngest brother.

LYNDE LORD. 1st.*

LYNDE LORD was a prominent patriot who was High Sheriff of Litchfield County, Connecticut, during 29. years and embracing the whole period of the Revolutionary War.

He was appointed Commissariat for purchasing supplies for the Connecticut troops, and was on various Committees to raise money for enlistments, and to stir up patriotism.

His name is mentioned nine times in an Historical Collection of the part sustained by Connecticut during the War. Showing that much of his time must have been devoted to the cause, without giving it actual military service.

See pages 176, 228, 256, 313, 373, 399, 447, 486, 514, "Hinman's War of the American Revolution."

*See Folio 13.

12

LORD. — LYNDE. — WILLOUGHBY. — PIERPONT.

WILLIAM LORD, son of Thomas Lord and Dorothy, his wife, born in London, England, in 1623., had by his first wife, (name unknown,)

Lieutenant RICHARD LORD,* born in Saybrooke, Conn., in 1647., died August 20.-1727., at Lyme, Conn. Married in 1682. Elizabeth Hyde, daughter of Samuel Hyde of Norwich, Conn., and Jane Lee, his wife. They had

Judge RICHARD LORD, born at Lyme, Conn., 1690., resided in Colony of Connecticut from 1690. to 1776. In 1720. he married Elizabeth Lynde. He died at Lyme, Conn., August 26.-1776., aged 86. years. He was Deputy from Lyme in 1729, & 30,-1732. & 33.-1735., 36 & 37.-1740., 1742. & 43.,-1746., 47. & 48.,-1752.-53.-54.-& 55.

ELIZABETH LYNDE, born December 2.-1704., married to Judge Richard Lord, 1720. died June 22.-1778. She was the daughter of Judge Nathaniel Lynde who was born in Boston, Mass., November 22.-1659., died October 5.-1729., and his wife Susannah Willoughby, whom he married at Boston, in 1683.

SUSANNAH WILLOUGHBY, was born, probably, at Charlestown, Mass., in 1664. and died February 2.-1710. She was the daughter of Francis Willoughby, born in England but resided in Charlestown, Mass., where he died April 4.-1671. He was Deputy Governor of the Colony of Massachusetts Bay, 1665. to 1670.

ENOCH LYNDE and ELIZABETH DIGBY, married October 25.-1614. in England. He died in London April 23.-1636. His estate was administered by his wife, who died October 7.-1636. They had

Judge SIMON LYNDE, baptised June 1624. at St. Andrew's, Holborn, Eng. He emigrated to America in 1650., married Hannah Newdigate February 1662. She was born December 20.-1624. He was Judge of Court of "Pleas and Sessions" July 21.-1686., Assistant Justice of Superior Court 1687., Member of Andros Council April 16.-1687, died November 22.-1687. They had

*See Folio 14.

LYNDE LORD.
1733--1801.

13

Judge NATHANIEL LYNDE, born in Boston, Mass. November 22.-
1659., resided in Boston, Mass., and Saybrooke, Conn., from
1659 to 1729. He was first Treasurer of Yale College, and
Deputy from Saybrooke to the General Court in 1691.-1698.-
1700.-1706.-1708.-1709.-1722. He married Susannah Willoughby at Boston in 1683, and died at Saybrooke October 5.-1729.
Their daughter, Elizabeth Lynde, born December 2.-1704.,
married to Judge Richard Lord in 1720. They had

LYNDE LORD, born at Litchfield, Conn., February 2.-1733., died
January 15.-1801., married July 7.-1757. Lois Sheldon. They
had

LYNDE LORD, Jr., born at Litchfield, Conn., October 21.-1762.,
married January 13.-1786., Mary Lyman, born 1764. Their
daughter
MARY SHELDON LORD, born January 30.-1787., married in
Litchfield, Conn., October 23.-1810., Rev. JOHN PIERPONT.

SHOWING DESCENT THROUGH HYDE AND COLLINS LINES

SAMUEL HYDE married JANE LEE	
They had,	
SAMUEL HYDE, JR. married ELIZABETH CALKINS, and had	ELIZABETH HYDE married LIEUT. RICHARD LORD and had
ELIZABETH HYDE married TIMOTHY COLLINS, and had	JANE LORD married SAMUEL ELY, and had
CHARLES COLLINS married ANNE HUNTINGDON, and had	ELIZABETH ELY married CAPT. ELISHA SHELDON, and had
ELIZABETH COLLINS married JAMES PIERPONT, and had	LOIS SHELDON married LYNDE LORD, and had
	LYNDE LORD, JR. married MARY LYMAN, and had
JOHN PIERPONT married MARY SHELDON LORD	

BROWN : WILLETT : HOOKER : PIERPONT

JOHN BROWN, born in England, 1584., resided at Boston, Mass. 1632., at Duxbury 1636., at Taunton 1643., died at Swanzey, April 10. 1662. He was Governor's Assistant, 1635.-1637 to 1655., 17 years. He was a Member of Council of War in Plymouth Colony, 1642.-1646. to 1653.; Commissioner of United Colonies from 1644. for 12. years; and a Purchaser of the "King's Province" (R. I.) in 1659. He married Dorothy —————, and had MARY BROWN, who married,

CAPT. THOMAS WILLETT, September 6.-1636. He was born in England in 1613., emigrated to America at the age of twenty years and resided in Massachusetts, Rhode Island, and New York from 1633. to 1674. He was Captain of Plymouth Train Band in 1647. Commissioner of Boundaries in 1650. Assistant Governor of Plymouth Colony in 1651. to 1664. Member of Governor's Council, N. Y., 1665. to 1672. Commissioner to go against the Dutch, June 20.-1654. Commissioner to organize His Majesty's Government in New York, 1665., Commissioner of Admiralty, August 23.-1665. First Mayor of New York City, 1667.-1668. They had a daughter, MARY WILLETT, who married

Rev. SAMUEL HOOKER, born at Cambridge, Mass., 1635., died at Farmington, Conn., November 6.-1697., married to Mary Willett, 1656. He graduated at Harvard, 1653. was Fellow of Harvard College, 1654., 1656., Pastor of Church at Farmington, 1661. to 1697., and preached Election Sermons, 1677., 1693. He was one of the Ministers active in forwarding the interests of the colony prior to 1675. He was the son of

Rev. THOMAS HOOKER, born in Leicestershire, England, July 7.-1586., died at Hartford, Conn., July 7.-1647., aged 61. years. He arrived in "The Griffin", September 4.-1633., and resided two and one-half years in Cambridge, Mass., where he was educated at Emanuel College. He was Minister of First Church of Hartford, Conn., 1636. to 1647., and was a recognized Founder of Connecticut.

MARY HOOKER, daughter of Rev. Samuel Hooker and Mary Willett, his wife, married, for his third wife, July 26.-1698.

Rev. JAMES PIERPONT, (XXII), born in Roxbury, Mass., Jan-

uary 4.-1659., graduated at Harvard, 1681. and settled in New
Haven, Conn., in 1685., and died there November 22.-1714.
He was Pastor of the First Church of New Haven from 1689.
to 1714., and preached the Election Sermon in 1690. He was
one of the Trustees named in the Act of 1701., "Establishing
a Collegiate School". This school was originally located at
Saybrooke, but was removed to New Haven in 1716., two years
after his death. From that date it has been known as Yale
College, of which he was a "Fellow" from 1701. to 1714. He
was father-in-law to Jonathan Edwards, who married his
daughter Sarah, and was a great friend of Cotton Mather.
He was the son of JOHN PIERPONT, (XXI), born in London,
England, 1619., married Thankful Stow, and settled near
Boston, Mass., in 1640. He was a Magistrate in that year,
and purchased in 1656. 300 acres of land, now the site of
Roxbury. He died December 7.-1682.

Rev. JAMES PIERPONT had by his third wife, MARY
HOOKER,

JAMES PIERPONT, Jr. (XXIII), born at New Haven, Conn.,
May 21.-1699., married Anna Sherman, March 28.-1758. They
had,

JAMES PIERPONT, 3d. (XXIV), born January 4.-1761.,
married September 24.-1782. Elizabeth Collins, who died
July 28.-1815. They had, for their second son,

REV. JOHN PIERPONT, born at Litchfield, Conn., April 6.-
1785.

DESCENDANTS OF JOHN PIERPONT (XXV)

(1) WILLIAM ALSTON PIERPONT. July, 11.-1811. Had one
daughter, MARY LORD, born at Watertown, N. Y., May 26.-
1838., married James Crosby, of Charlestown, N. H., son
of Jaazaniah Crosby and Huldah Robinson Sage, of Charlestown, N. H. He was born September 23.-1820. and died in
Boston, Mass., October 27.-1896. She died in Boston, March
27.-1913. They had two children

(a) JAMES ALLEN CROSBY, born July 28.-1864., at Boston,
Mass. He married, on September 25.-1912, Susan Lillian
Bartlett, daughter of Joseph Alves Bartlett and Sarah Ella
Black, who were married April 10.-1877. She was born Sep-

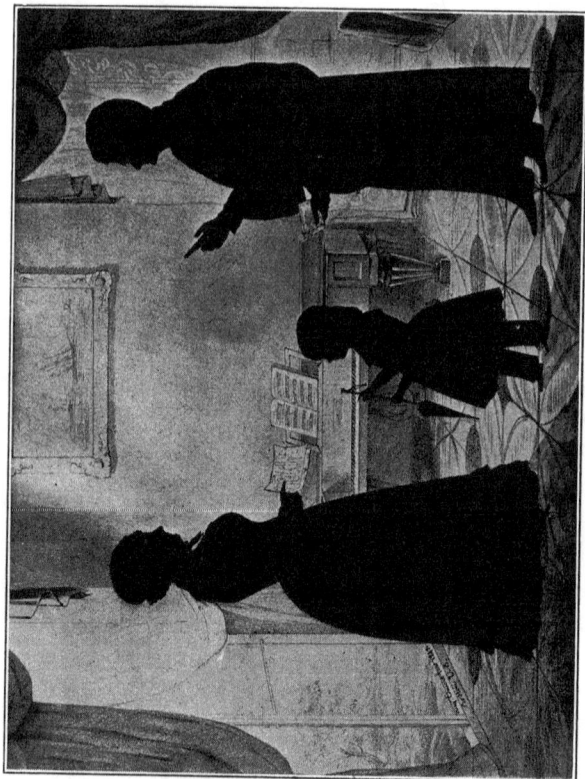

REV. JOHN PIERPONT, MRS. PIERPONT,
AND MARY LORD PIERPONT

(MRS. JAMES CROSBY).

17

tember 25.-1880.
(b) MARY PIERPONT, born in West Roxbury, Mass., June 22.-
1869., and married November 1.-1896., to Edward Webster
McGlenen, son of Henry Aloysius McGlenen and Caroline
Matilda Bruce, born July 11.-1854., in Boston, Mass. They
had two sons
HENRY ALLEN McGLENEN, born in Boston, Mass., April
6.-1897., married April 17.-1926., Madeline Doris, born November 11.-1900., at Rockland, Mass., daughter of William
Henry Mack and Florence Stanley, who married November 1.-
1899. He died in 1904.
EDWARD WEBSTER McGLENEN, Jr., born in Boston, Mass.,
May 20.-1898. Ordained and Installed Minister of the First
Parish Church at Brewster, Mass., October 24.-1926. Married
at Christ Church, Dorchester, November 29.-1926., Alice Irene,
daughter of Mr. and Mrs. Waldo Traffarn Whitney. She was
born February 28.-1903.
(A Hymn sung at his Ordination was written by his Great-
great-grandfather, Rev. John Pierpont.)

THE MORGAN LINE

P.XXV.3 JULIET PIERPONT, born July 30.-1816. married May
2.-1836. to JUNIUS SPENCER MORGAN, born April 14.-
1813., died April 8.-1890. She died February 23.-1884.
Mr. Morgan was of Hartford, Conn., but later associated with
the Banking-house of Peabody & Morgan of London, England,
where he resided many years. Their children were
M.1. John Pierpont Morgan, born April 17.-1837., died in Rome,
Italy, March 31.-1913.
M.2. Sarah Spencer, born December 5.-1839., died July 5.-1896.
M.3. Mary Lyman, born November 5.-1844., died July 20.-1919.
M.4. Junius Spencer Morgan, Jr. born April 6.-1846., died March
12.-1858.
M.5. Juliet Pierpont, born December 4.-1847., died April 1.-1923.

JOHN PIERPONT MORGAN.

Born April 17.-1837., died March 31.-1913.

Mr. Morgan was America's leading financier of International fame, and head of the well known Banking-houses of J. P. Morgan & Co., of New York, Drexel, Morgan & Co. of Philadelphia, Morgan, Grenfeld & Co. of London, Morgan, Harjes & Co. of Paris. He was also a noted collector of books, paintings and articles of virtu, and the generous donation of his Library, Miniatures and other works of art to the public constitutes his most precious monument.

In 1861. he married his first wife, Amelia Sturges, who died February 1862., without issue.

In 1865. he married his second wife, Frances Louisa Tracy, born May 15.-1842., died November 16.-1924. Their children were

M.1.A. Louisa Pierpont, born March 10.-1866.

M.1.B. John Pierpont Morgan, II, born September 7.-1867.

M.1.C. Juliet Pierpont, born July 17.-1870.

M.1.D. Anne Tracy, born July 25.-1873.

M.2. SARAH SPENCER MORGAN, born December 5.-1839. died July 5.-1896. married June 27.-1866. George Hale Morgan, born February 14.-1840., who died April 28.-1911. Their children were

M.2.A. JUNIUS SPENCER MORGAN, born June 5.-1867., married June 4.-1891. Josephine A. Perry, born October 21.-1869., by whom he had

   a. SARAH SPENCER, Jr., born February 17.-1893., married September 12.-1914. Henry B. Gardner by whom she had:—SARAH MORGAN, born July 30.-1915.

   b. ALEXANDER PERRY MORGAN, born October 23.-1900., married February 10.-1923. Janet S. Croll, born January 28.-1901., by whom he had

   c. LUCRETIA PERRY, died in infancy.

   d. ALEXANDER PERRY MORGAN, JR., born May 8.-1924.

   e. MARGARET CROLL, born November 30.-1926.

M.2.B. GEORGE DENISON MORGAN, born June 17.-1876., died July 9.-1915., married Yuki Kato, January 21.-1904.

M.2.C. CAROLINE LUCY, born March 4.-1873.

M.3. MARY LYMAN MORGAN, born November 5.-1844., died

REV. JOHN PIERPONT AT 60.

July 20.-1919., married January, 1867. Walter Hayes Burns born September 9.-1838., died November 22.-1897., by whom she had

M.3.A. MARY ETHEL, born October 21.-1873, married July 1.-1899, Lewis Harcourt, (1st Viscount) born January 31.-1863 who died February 24.-1922. Their children were

a. DORIS, M. T. born March 30.-1900., married, Nov. 17.-1924., Hon. Alexander Francis St. Vincent Baring, born April 7.-1898.

b. OLIVIA VERNON, born April 5.-1902., married, October 29.-1923., Hon. Godfrey John M. L. Mulholland, born October 3.-1892., by whom she had MARY NORAH, born October 23.-1924.

c. BARBARA, born April 28.-1905., married, July 25.-1925., Robert Charles I. Jenkinson, born December 2.-1900., by whom she had JULIAN C. L. JENKINSON, born April 28.-1926.

d. Hon. WILLIAM EDWARD HARCOURT, (2nd Viscount), born October 5.-1908.

M.3.B. WALTER S. M. BURNS, born March 22.-1872., married February 9.-1907. Ruth Evelyn Cavendish Bentinck, born March 5.-1883., by whom he had

a. CYNTHIA MARY, born January 22.-1908.

b. WALTER A. G. BURNS, born January 29.-1911.

M.5. JULIET PIERPONT MORGAN, born December 4.-1847., died April 1.-1923., married July 11.-1871. Rev. John B. Morgan, born March 4.-1843., died January 12.-1912. By whom she had

M.5.A. Ursula J., born October 26.-1873., died February 5.-1916., married June,-1908. William Fitz Simon. No issue.

M.5.B. John Junius Morgan, born April 26.-1876., married October 6.-1908, Caroline A. McCook, born May 31.-1887. No issue living, a boy died in infancy.

M.1.A. LOUISA PIERPONT MORGAN, born March 10.-1866., married November 15.-1900., Herbert L. Satterlee, born October 31.-1863., by whom she had

a. Mabel M., born August 13.-1901., married September 19.-1926., Francis Abbott Ingalls, Jr., born February 19.-1895.

b. Eleanor M., born April 12.-1905.

20

M.1.B. JOHN PIERPONT MORGAN, II., born September 7.-
1867., married December 11.-1890. Jane Norton Grew, born
September 30.-1868., died August 14.-1925. Their children are
a. Junius Spencer Morgan, Jr., born March 15.-1892.
b. Jane Norton, born November 14.-1893.
c. Frances Tracy, born January 17.-1897.
d. Henry Sturgis Morgan, born October 24.-1900.
M.1.B.a. JUNIUS SPENCER MORGAN, Jr. married, June 15,-
1915. Louise Converse born April 1.-1895. Their children
are
Louise Converse Morgan, Jr., born January 15.-1917.
John Pierpont Morgan, Jr., born June 1.-1918.
Anne Morgan, born September 28.-1922.
M.1.B.b. JANE NORTON MORGAN, married, November 14.-
1917., George Nichols, born October 14.-1878. Their children
are
Jane Norton Nichols, Jr., born September 8.-1918.
George Nichols, Jr., born May 15.-1922.
Henrietta Mary, born March 6.-1927.
M.1.B.c. FRANCES TRACY MORGAN, married, June 16.-1917.,
Paul Geddes Pennoyer, born October 30.-1890. Their children
are
Virginia M. Pennoyer, born March 17.-1918.
Paul G. Pennoyer, Jr., born February 11.-1920.
Frances T. Pennoyer, born June 1.-1921.
Katherine E. Pennoyer, born April 9.-1925.
Robert Morgan Pennoyer, born April 9.-1925.
Jessie Morgan Pennoyer, born August 12.-1926.
M.1.B.d. HENRY STURGIS MORGAN, married, June 26.-1923.,
Catherine Adams, born January 13.-1902. Their children are
Henry S. Morgan, Jr., born August 10.-1924.
Charles Francis Morgan, born April 16.-1926.

M.1.C. JULIET PIERPONT MORGAN, born July 17.-1870.,
married, April 1894., William Pierson Hamilton, born February 5.-1869. Their children are
a. Helen Morgan, born June 12.-1896.
b. Pierpont Morgan Hamilton, born August 3.-1898.
c. Laurens M. Hamilton, born June 18.-1900.
d. Alexander Hamilton, born January 25.-1903.

e. Elizabeth S. Hamilton, born December 19.-1907., died
January 3.-1919.

M.l.C.a. HELEN MORGAN HAMILTON, married, June 10.-1916.,
Arthur Woods, born January 29.-1870. Their children are
John Pierpont Woods, born February 6.-1918.
Leonard H. Woods, born October 15.-1919.
Alexander Hamilton Woods, born July 26.-1922.
Caroline F., born March 1.-1927.

M.l.C.b. PIERPONT MORGAN HAMILTON, married September
11.-1919., Marie Louise Blair, born July 1.-1899. Their chil-
dren are
Philip Schuyler Hamilton, born November 21.-1920.
David Blair Hamilton, born July 20.-1922.
Ian Morgan Hamilton, born October 4.-1923.

M.l.C.c. LAURENS M. HAMILTON, married, January 22.-1920.,
Mrs. Gregory Warren.

XXV. JOHN PIERPONT, (Rev.) Continued.*

XXVI. (5.) JAMES LORD PIERPONT, born in Boston, Mass.,
April 25.-1822., died at Winter-Haven, Fla., August, 1893.,
buried in Savannah, Ga. Married, first, in Troy, N. Y.,
September 4.-1846., Millicent Cowee, daughter of Farwell
Cowee and Abigail Merriam, born in Westminster, Mass.,
June 22.-1822., died at West Medford, Mass., the home of
Rev. John Pierpont, August 17.-1856., and is buried in
Mt. Auburn Cemetery, Cambridge, Mass. Their children
were

(A.) MARY AUGUSTA, born August 20.-1847. at Troy, N. Y.

(B.) JOHN PIERPONT, born August 11.-1849. at Troy,
N. Y,. died at Milwaukee, Wis., December 6.-1879.

(C.) JOANNA LE BARRON, born March, 1855. at West
Medford, Mass., died August 23.-1855, at West Medford,
Mass.

JAMES PIERPONT afterward married, in Savannah, Ga., Eliza
Jane Purse, born 1833., died in Winter Haven, Fla., May
4.-1889. Their children were

(D.) LILIAN PURSE, born in Savannah, Ga.

(E.) JAMES PIERPONT, Jr., born in Savannah, Ga., died at
six months of age.

*See Folio 9.

(F.) THOMAS PURSE PIERPONT, Savannah, Ga., born November 3.-1862. died November 1.-1891.

(G.) JURIAH HARRIS PIERPONT, Savannah, Ga., born February 25.-1864.

(H.) MAYNARD BOARDMAN PIERPONT, born at Valdosta, Ga., November 17.-1866. Married Clara A. Crouch in Richmond, Va., May 17.-1887., died at Pensacola, Fla., July 17.-1897.

XXVI. DESCENDANTS OF JAMES PIERPONT

THEO. F. BARNUM LINE

(A) MARY AUGUSTA, born at Troy, N. Y., August 20.-1847., married at Troy, October 12.-1870., to Theodore Frelinghuysen Barnum, son of Milo Barnum and Rebecca Byoughton, his wife, was born at Dresden, N. Y., October 12.-1844., died at Troy, N. Y., August 31.-1918. (Milo Barnum was born in Danbury, Conn., June 14.-1808., died in Troy, N. Y., January 6.-1890., and Rebecca Byoughton was born in Danbury, June 8.-1808. and died in Troy, N. Y., March.-1899. They were married in Danbury, January 6.-1832.) Their children were

(a) Louise, born in Troy, N. Y., December 19.-1872., died July 1.-1873.

(b) Theodore Pierpont Barnum, born in Troy, N. Y., March 26.-1874.

(c) Millicent Cowee, born at Troy, October 26.-1877., died July 8.-1883.

(d) John Pierpont Barnum, born at Troy, July 14.-1884.

(e) David Farwell Barnum, born at Troy, November 9.-1886.

(b) THEODORE PIERPONT BARNUM, married in Troy, N. Y., April 18.-1900., Antoinette Spencer Alden, daughter of Charles L. Alden and Mary Langford Taylor, born in Troy, N. Y., May 29.-1871. (Charles L. Alden was born at Lewis, Essex Co., N. Y., August 21.-1827., and died at Dorchester, Mass., November, 1902. His wife was born at Westmoreland, Oneida Co., N. Y., August 16.-1846., and died at Little Compton, R. I., May 20.-1923.) Their daughter
Mary Alden, born in Troy, N. Y., December 31.-1905.

(d) JOHN PIERPONT BARNUM, married at Omaha, Neb., June 16.-1910., Dorothy Hansen. Their children are
Dorothy, born at Omaha, January 20.-1912.

Betty, born at Omaha, April 20.-1914.

John Pierpont Barnum, Jr., born at Brooklyn, N. Y., June 22.-1917.

(e) DAVID FARWELL BARNUM, married at Omaha, Neb., May 29.-1918., Hulda Hansen. Adopted ROBERT FARWELL, born April 2.-1920.

XXVII. JOHN PIERPONT, son of James, born August 11.-1849., at Troy, N. Y., married in Chicago, October 22.-1873., Ellen Ryan McGregor, of Milwaukee, Wis. They had two children
(a) Antoinette, born August 21.-1874.
(b) David Cowee Pierpont, born December 6.-1878. (XXVIII.)

(a) ANTOINETTE, born August 21.-1874., married Joseph Cary James, son of Garth Wilkinson James and Caroline Eames Cary. He died September 10.-1925. *They had one son, Garth Pierpont, born January 16-1909.*

XXVIII.
(b) DAVID COWEE PIERPONT, M. D., born December 4.-1878., married Aya Marsh. Their children are
(1) John Pierpont, born August 21.-1914. (XXIX.)
(2) David Pierpont, Jr., born July 6.-1916.
(3) William Marsh Pierpont, born November 22.-1917.
(4) James Pierpont, born April 18.-1920.

(7) JURIAH HARRIS PIERPONT, M. D., born in Savannah, Ga., February 25.-1864., married in Pensacola, Fla., August 21.-1894., Lucy Penelope Warren. Their children are
(a) Frances Tracy, born in Pensacola, Fla., May 19.-1895., died May 20.-1895.
(b) Margery, born in Pensacola, Fla., November 12.-1901.
(c) Florence Frances, born in Pensacola, Fla., March 7.-1903.
(d) Andrew Warren Pierpont, born in Pensacola, Fla., February 13.-1906.

(8) MAYNARD BOARDMAN PIERPONT, born in Valdosta, Ga., November 17.-1866., married, in Richmond, Va., May 17.-1887., Clara A. Crouch. He died in Pensacola, Fla., July 17.-1897. Their children are
(a) Robert Crouch Pierpont, born March 12.-1888.
(b) Lucile, born in Winter Haven, Fla., December 14.-1889.,

died in Atlanta, Ga., June 10.-1914.

(c) Julia Tebeau, born December 31.-1891., married, September 6.-1925., Phillip Christian, Jr. Died April 29.-1926. in Atlanta, Ga.

(d) James Morgan Pierpont, born in Winter Haven, Fla., October 21.-1894., died June, 1897.

(a) ROBERT CROUCH PIERPONT, born March 12.-1888., married August 10.-1910, Myrtle Duffill, daughter of Cicero Franklin Duffill, of Jonesboro, Ga., and Rose Ella Sanders, his wife. Their children are

(1) Lilian, born in Atlanta, Ga., November 27.-1911.

REV. SAMUEL PIERPONT.

On the dunes of Wannatawket, now Fisher's Island, at the east end, near the East Beach, a few feet only from where the billows of the Great Atlantic daily encroach and recede, there is a lonely grave, marked by a massive table-monument of brownstone on which are engraved these words:—

HERE LIES THE BODY OF Ye Rd. Mr.

SAMUEL PIERPONT, PASTOR of
Ye
FIRST CH. in LYME, SON of Ye Rd.

Mr. JAMES PIERPONT of NEW HAVEN,

WHO WAS BORN DEC. 30. 1700. &

DROWNED MARCH 15. 1722/3. PASSING

THE CONNECTICUT RIVER ABOVE

SAYBROOK FERRY AND THE

28. of APRIL 1723.

WAS FOUND HERE.

He was brother to Sarah Pierpont who married Jonathan Edwards and grandson to Samuel Hooker of Farmington. He was the second son of Rev. James Pierpont and his third wife, "Sweet Mary Hooker," and graduated from Yale College in 1718. He went to Lyme February 16.–1720/1. as lay preacher under Rev. Moses Noyes, at the First Church, and was ordained there December 12.–1772., when he became Pastor.

(From newspaper clipping.)

DESCENT THROUGH ELIZABETH LYNDE FROM ALFRED THE GREAT, who had

2 Ethelinda, married Baldwin II, Ct. of Flanders, had
3 John de Burgo, Earl Comyn, Baron Foulgues, had
4 Harlamen de Burgo who had
5 Robt. de Burgh, Earl of Cornwall and Moreton, had
6 Wm. de Burgh, de Moreton, Earl of Cornwall who rebelled against Henry II and had his eyes plucked out by his order, had
7 John de Burgh, had
8 Herbert de Burgh, Earl of Kent, Chief Justice of Ireland and England and guardian of Henry III. Died 1243. He married Lady Beatrix, daughter of William de Warren, Ld., of Wiamegay, had
9 Sir John, Baron de Burgh, who married Lady Harvise, daughter of Wm. Baron de Lanvallee', one of the twenty-five Magna Charta barons, and had
10 John de Burgh, Baron de Lanvallee, had
11 Lady Hanysi de Burgh, married Robert, Baron de Gresliv of Kingston and Portesdale, died 1283; they had,
12 Lady Joan de Gresliv, who married John de la Warre, they had,
13 Lady Catherine de la Warre, married Sir W. de Latimer, Knt., second son of Baron Latimer of Braybrooke who died, 1350. They had
14 Lady Elizabeth Latimer who married Sir Thomas Griffin, Knt., of Weston, Lord North Hampton and had
15 Richard Griffin who married Anne, daughter of Richard Chamberlain and had
16 Nicholas Griffin, second son, of Nottinghamshire, who married Catherine, daughter of John Curson and had
17 Lady Catherine Griffin, married Sir John Digby of Eye Kettleby, Leicestershire, had
18 Wm. Digby of Kettleby who married Rose Perwich of Perwich and had
19 Simon Digby of Bedale, Ruplonidshire, married Anne, daughter of Reginald Grey, Yorkshire, had
20 Everard Digby, married Catherine, daughter of Magister Stockbridge de Vandershoff, Sher. of New Kirk, they had
21 Elizabeth Digby, born 1584, who married Enoch Lynde of

London and had

22 Simon Lynde of Boston, born 1624, died 1687, came to New England 1650. He was made Judge. He married Hannah, daughter of John Newgate, London, had,

23 Nathaniel Lynde of Saybrooke, Conn., born 1659, died 1729. Was first Treasurer of the college school of Saybrooke. Married in 1683, Susannah, daughter of Francis Willoughby, Deputy Governor of Massachusetts Colony 1665 to -71. She died 1709. They had

24 Elizabeth Lynde who married Judge Richard Lord of Lyme, Conn. She was born 169- died 1776. Had

25 Lynde Lord, married Lois Sheldon and had

26 Lynde Lord, Jr., married Mary Lyman, had

27 Mary Sheldon Lord, married John Pierpont.

DESCENT FROM WILLIAM THE CONQUEROR THROUGH JAMES PIERPONT.

1 William the Conqueror, who had

2 Lady Gundreda, who married Wm. de Warren, Earl of Surrey, they had

3 William, second Earl of Warren and Surrey, died 1131, and had

4 Lady Isabel Warren who married Rogoer Bigod Earl of Norfolk, had

5 Hugh Bigod, Earl of Norfolk, married Lady Furnival, they had

6 Ralph, third son, who had

7 Isabel Bigod, who married John Fitz Piers Fitz Goeffrey, Ld. of Berhampshed, Chief Justice of Ireland 1246, and had

8 John Fitz John, C. J. of Ireland 1258, he had

9 Lady Maud Fitz John, who married secondly Wm. 6th Baron Beauchamp, Earl of Warwick, had

10 Guy, 2nd Earl of Warwick, who married Lady Alice, daughter of Ralph, Baron de Tabi, had

11 Thomas, 3rd Earl of Warwick, one of the original Knights of the Garter who married Lady Catherine Mortimer, daughter of Roger, Earl of Marche, had

12 Thomas, 4th Earl of Warwick, married Lady Margaret, daughter of William, 3rd Lord Torrens; they had

13 Richard, 5th Earl of Warwick and Earl of Albemarle, K.G., High Steward of England, Lieut. Governor of Normandy;

Guardian of Henry VI. He married Lady Elizabeth Berkeley, daughter of Thomas 12th Baron Berkeley and had

14 Lady Margaret Beauchamp married secondly Sir William Cavendish, had

15 Thomas Cavendish, Knt. who was Clerk of the pipe in the Exchequer under Henry VIII, died 1524; married Alice Smith, daughter of John Smith of Padbrooke Hall, Suffolk;—

16 William Cavendish, Knt. of Chatamarble, Gentleman Usher of Cardinal Wolsey and the King's Privy Councillor and Treasurer. Died 153?, married Lady Elizabeth Hardwicke, daughter of John Hardwicke, had

17 Lady Frances Cavendish who married Sir Henry Pierpont, Knt., they had

18 Wm. Pierpont, who married Elizabeth of Lancastire, had

19 James Pierpont, married Margaret, had

20 John, who had by Thankful Stowe

21 James, founder of Yale College, who married Mary Hooker, they had

22 James, married Anna Sherman, they had

23 James, married Elizabeth Collins, they had

24 John, married May Sheldon Lord.

BOARDMAN GENEALOGY

I. WILLIAM BOREMAN, of Banbury, Oxfordshire, England. His name is found in a Lay Subsidy list for Banbury Hundred, (a division, or circuit,) in the 16th. year of the reign of Henry VIII. (1525.) "Will. BOREMAN, Banbury, In Bonis, 40s. 7d. (his tax on goods.)" His birth and death are not recorded.

II. THOMAS BOREMAN, "the elder", of CLAYDON, near Banbury, son of William (1), is the first of the name found in that town, and is mentioned in a Lay Subsidy list for Banbury Hundred in 1546, and is taxed £3. 0s.3d. on goods. The Parish Register of Claydon begins in 1569, ten years before the death of Thomas; hence the baptisms of his children are not to be found in it, and their names can be gathered only from his will, dated April 3.-1576, and which was proved May 2.-1580, his death occurring December 9.-1579. He appears to have been a farmer in good circumstances. His wife, named Isabell, survived him, but there is no record of her death. His children were

1. William, married Annis, (?) buried January 10.-1612-13.
2. Cicely, or Sisley, married John Russell, May 8.-1576.
3. Christopher, buried October 10.-1584.
4. John, ———— buried December 9.-1588.
5. Thomas, the elder, married Alice; buried May 29.-1593.
6. Thomas, the younger, married Dorothy Gregory, February 16.-1579-80.
7. Elizabeth, married November 17.-1584, Thomas Symkins, no record of burial.
8. Joan, may have been one of two Joan Boremans, who married respectively Humphrey Welch, November 24.-1585, and John Mason, June 10.-1585.
9. Ann, buried January 21.-1575-6, probably quite young.

BOARDMAN.
COAT OF ARMS.

(Note,—The double dates, necessary to bring them to the new style which begins the year with January 1st. instead of April 1st.)

III. WILLIAM BOREMAN, of Claydon, grandfather of Thomas Boreman of Ipswich, Mass., baptism not recorded, married Annis ———, who died about five years before her husband and was buried May 12th.-1608. Their children had then all been married, and William afterwards made his home with his eldest son, Thomas, another son, John, perhaps living in the same house. The three remaining sons, Nicholas, William, and Christopher, do not appear in the Claydon Register, and probably settled elsewhere. The will of William was made December 12.-1610, and it was proved April 13.-1613. He was buried January 10.-1612-13, aged probably not far from 60 years. His inventory, taken on the day of his burial, indicates that he was in comfortable circumstances with an estate larger than his father's. His occupation seems to have been exclusively husbandry. His children were

1. Thomas, married Elizabeth Carter, February 2.-1595-6, buried March 9.-1627-8.
2. Nicholas,—probably removed.
3. William,—probably removed.
4. John, married Elizabeth Poley, June 25.-1593.
5. Annis, married ——— Claridge.
6. Allice, married Walter Poley, October 25.-1584; and 2nd. ——— Brown.
7. Jone, baptized May 20.-1570, married Edward Haynes, September 27.-1596.
8. Christopher, baptized January 16.-1572-3; probably removed.

IV. THOMAS BOREMAN, eldest son of William and Annis, and father of Thomas, the emigrant to Ipswich, Mass., was born about 1570. married, on February 2nd.-1595-6, Elizabeth, eldest daughter of Felix and Margaret Carter, who was born about 1575. Thomas died at about 58 years of age and was buried March 9th.-1627-8. His property considerably exceeded that of his father, William, and of his grandfather, Thomas. His widow, Elizabeth, continued to manage it until her death three years later, when at the age of 56, and in that short time the value of the property more than doubled in her competent hands. She was buried May 11.-1631. A special interest attaches to the study of the position and circumstances of this family, from the fact that their emigrant son, Thomas, was one of those honored through life in New England by the then rare title of "Mr!" The children of Thomas and Elizabeth Boreman were

1. William, baptized November 20.-1596; buried March 10.-1612-13, aged 17. years. Since he died so young the habit of naming the eldest sons alternately William and Thomas was broken and seems not to have been renewed.
2. Felix, baptized March 4.-1598-9.; settled in London.
3. THOMAS, baptized October 18.-1601; married Margaret ————, and with her, emigrated to New England and settled at Ipswich, Mass.
4. Samuel, baptized February 4.-1603-4; probably died young, not mentioned in his father's will.
5. Daniel, baptized March 21.-1605-6; unmarried and living with his brother Thomas in New England as late as December 1670.
6. John, baptized October 30.-1608.; buried September 3.-1680.
7. Joseph, baptized April 17.-1611; married ————, lived not far from London.
8. Job, baptized December 18.-1613; died an apprentice in London; buried October 1.-1632.
9. Sarah, baptized May 4.-1617. no further record.

V. THOMAS BOREMAN, the emigrant to Ipswich, Mass., was born in Claydon, baptized there October 18.-1601. Nothing has been found in English records to show where he lived just before his emigration. We infer from the fact that his mother's bequest to him in her will of 1631. was, like that of his brother Felix, in money only, that he was not then, at the age of 30., living in Claydon. He must somewhere have learned in his youth his trade of cooper. The exact date of Thomas Boreman's coming to

New England is not known. He was probably here as early as 1634, but is first found on record in March 1634-5, when he was made freeman by the General Court of Massachusetts. His first grant of land is recorded at Ipswich in 1635. "Granted to Thomas Boreman about fifty-five acres of land, x x x also a six acre lott on the northeast side the Hill by the towne, Likewise an house-lott in the Towne, upon which he has built an house, having Mr. Bartholomew on the southwest. To enjoy to him and his heirs and assigns forever." The piece of fifty-five acres is in the second entry described as, "An Island about fifty-five acres of land, meadow and upland, bounded on the north and northeast by a creek parting it and an Island belonging to John Perkins, the Elder, and on the south a' p'sell of land formerly granted to George Carr, and on the west the great creek called Labour in vayne."

To establish communication with the town a bridge was necessary, and this Thomas Boreman built. The Island was, in the third generation thereafter, the property of Thomas' grandson, Jacob Bordman, who, by deed of gift, dated June 23d. 1748, gave it to his two sons, Jacob and John. The bridge there is to this day called by his name, and the street leading to it, for the most part a country road, is named Boardman Street.

The family name of Thomas Boreman's wife, Margaret, has not been found, neither does it appear whether they were married before or after coming to New England. Judging from what can be gathered as to the ages of their children, it seems probable that their marriage took place not long before leaving England, at which time Thomas was about 33 years old and his wife no doubt considerably younger; her surviving him some seven years would indicate this. Her title of Mrs. or Mistress, implies the respectability of her family. If their family all lived to maturity, their number was not a large one for that day. It should not be forgotten that their family included also Thomas Boreman's brother Daniel, who lived to be at least 65. and who, although he makes no figure in Ipswich records, is to Thomas Boreman's descendants a most im-

portant personage, without the knowledge of whose exist-
ence they would have no certainty. of their English
ancestry. Particular attention should be given to a clause
in Thomas Boreman's will, providing for his brother
Daniel, which, in connection with a similar clause in the
will of his mother, Elizabeth Boreman of Claydon, fully
proves Thomas Boreman's origin.

Thomas Boreman's will, (original on file in the Probate
Office in Salem,) was made December 17.-1670, when he
was past his 69th. year. He made a codicil dated May 3d.-
1673, and his inventory was taken on the 26th. of the
same month, showing that he died in May, 1673, aged
72 years and 7 months. (It is interesting to note that his
cousin, Samuel Boreman of Westfield, Conn., fourteen
years younger, had died in April, about one month before.) Mrs. Margaret Boreman, the widow, died November 25th.-1679. (Essex Co. Records, Salem.)

It should here be noted that a gradual change in the
spelling of the name took place about this time. The
will of Thomas shows, in his signature, that he spelled
his name BORMAN, leaving out the E in the middle. His
widow also spells her name BORMAN in her will, but
letters from friends spell it either Boreman or Bourman,
while the street, bridge, and Island, named for him, are
BOARDMAN. Children of Thomas and Margaret were

1. Mary, married Robert Kinsman, Jr., born 1629.
2. Daniel, married April 12.-1662, Hannah, daughter
   of Richard and Alice Hutchinson of Salem, born
   January 20.-1639, died in Topsfield, April 27.-1708.
3. Martha, married July 4.-1660, Deacon Thomas Low.
4. THOMAS, born 1643, married January 1.-1667-8,
   Elizabeth, daughter of Sargt. Jacob Perkins, born
   April 1.-1650. He died October 3.-1719, in his
   76th year. His wife died December 4.-1718, aged
   68 years 8. mos. 3. da. Gravestone in Ipswich.
5. Joanna, married January 29.-1672, Isaac Fellows.
   She was born in 1635, and died March 20.-1732, in
   her 86th. year.

VI. The children of THOMAS and ELIZABETH were

33

1. Thomas, born August 8.-1669, married Sarah Langley.
2. Jacob, born June 10.-1671; married Martha, widow of John Rogers, in 1699.
3. John, born March 18.-1672, no further record.
4. OFFIN, born December 3.-1676, married Sarah Heard, February 28.-1698.
5. Margaret, born April.-1681, married Thomas Burnham,-1703.
6. Elizabeth, born November 9.-1686, married Jedediah Tittcomb,-1717.

VII. OFFIN BORDMAN, (No. 4. above,) of Salisbury, Innkeeper, married Sarah Heard, February 28.-1698. Two children are recorded to them in Ipswich, Offin and Nathaniel. The will of this Offin, made January 1747, proved April 2.-1750, mentions Judith "my now loving wife," and grandsons Offin, Thomas, Jacob, John, Jonathan, and grand-daughter Elizabeth Pearson, children of son Offin, deceased; also grandchildren Amos, Stephen, John, Sarah, and Elizabeth Coffin, orphan children of his daughter, Sarah Coffin.

VIII. OFFIN BOARDMAN, born December 16.-1698; married Sarah Woodman. He was Master of a vessel, which, in going from Casco Bay to Boston with a cargo of rafts at her stern, was overset, September-1735, and he with twelve others were drowned! (History of Newbury,) His children were †Offin, Elizabeth (married John Pearson in 1748.) Thomas, John, Jacob and Jonathan, as mentioned by his father. His widow married Stephen Wyatt.

IX. *JONATHAN BOARDMAN, born March 15.-1735, married in Newbury, March 12.-1761, Rebecca Moody. Their descendants are living in Calais, Maine, and Macon, Ga., and elsewhere. The old Bible belonging to Jonathan has these entries, without names, but evidently relating to Offin and his wife, Sarah, afterwards wife of Stephen Wyatt:—

*See Folio 34.   †See Folio 40.

"Sept. 8,-1735, my honored father departed this life."
"July 12,-1752, my honored mother departed this life."

The foregoing facts are taken from the "BOARDMAN
GENEALOGY", 1525-1895, compiled by Charlotte Gold-
thwaite, and published by William F. J. Boardman, at
Hartford, Conn., Press of the Case, Lockwood & Brainard
Company, in 1895.

The sincere gratitude of the entire Boardman family is
due Mr. William F. J. Boardman and Mrs. Charlotte
Goldthwaite, for the prodigious labor intelligently exerted,
the great length of time and large amount of money
expended in procuring the data and publishing these facts
in such a complete and satisfactory manner. Mrs. Goldthwaite's co-operation in compiling them so attractively
is deserving of high commendation.

Mr. Boardman, being more directly interested in that
branch of the family descending from Samuel Boreman
of Wethersfield, Conn., naturally did not prolong the in-
vestigation among those descending from Thomas Boreman, of Ipswich, Mass., farther than this point; but he
indicates the direction in which inquiries should be made,
and leaves comparatively little for those to do whom may
desire to pursue the subject farther.

*Jonathan Boardman, in the History of Newburyport,
folio 124, is mentioned as one of the founders of King
Cyrus Chapter of Royal Arch Masons, in 1790.

X. JONATHAN BOARDMAN, Jr. Son of Jonathan and Rebecca Moody, baptized in Newburyport, Mass., February
27.-1780. (Church Record, Vol. 3.) Married in Newburyport, December 26.-1804. to Sarah Horton.

XI. JOSEPH M. BOARDMAN, son of Jonathan, Jr., and Sarah
Horton, born at Newburyport, Mass., May 10th.-1808.
Died June 28th.-1893. at Macon, Ga. Married, 1., Maria
Theresa Lord, daughter of Joseph Lynde Lord, born Feb-
ruary 25th.-1805., died at Macon, Ga. July 12th.-1847.
S. P.

Married, 2., Caroline Augusta Pierpont, the mother of
his children, on September 27th.-1848., daughter of Rev.

JOSEPH M. BOARDMAN.
1808—1893.

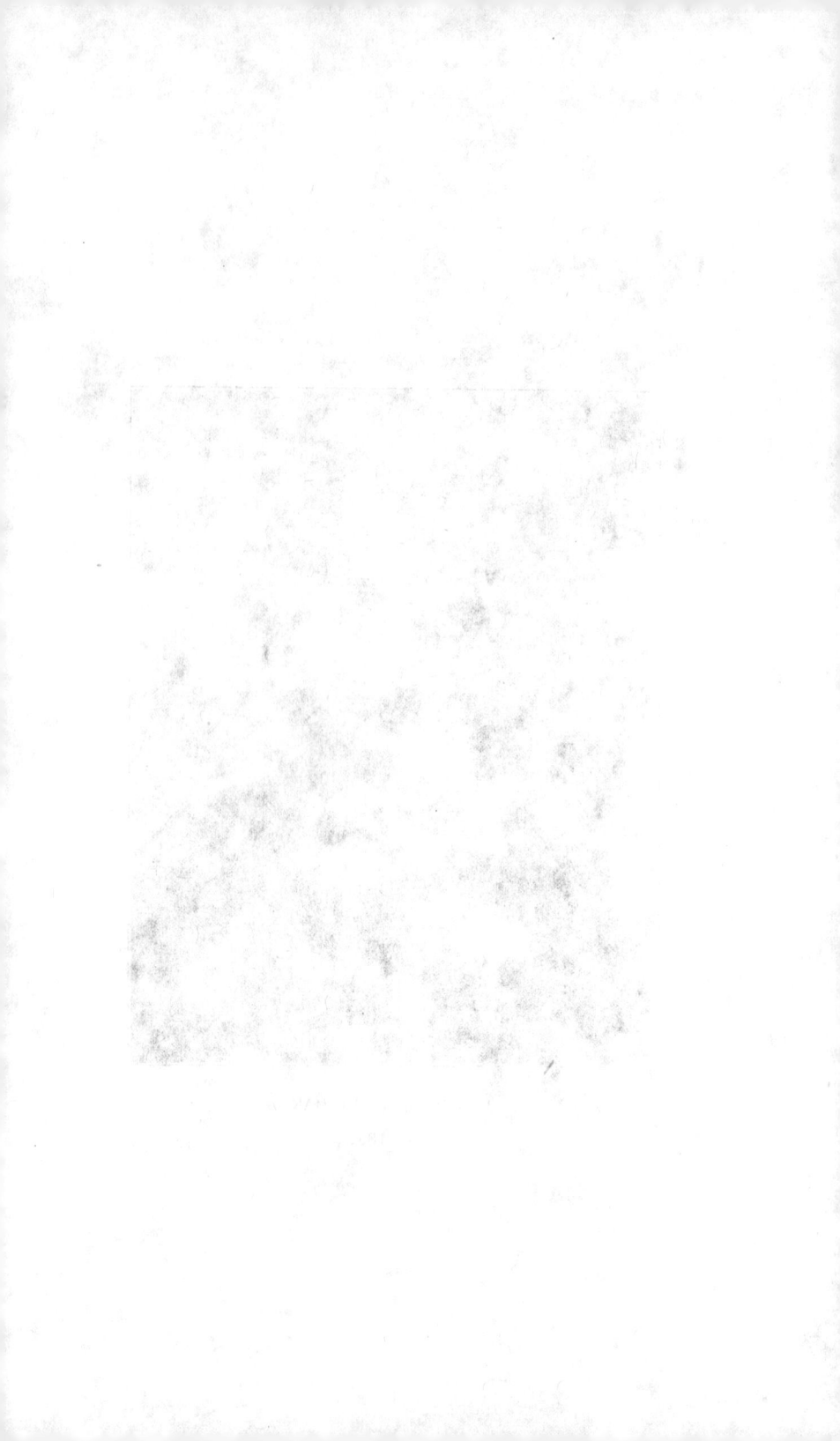

John Pierpont and Mary Sheldon Lord. Born August 21st.-1823., at Boston, Mass. Died at Macon, Ga., September 17th.-1881.

Married, 3., at Macon, Ga., October-1882., Elodia Billings Trapp, widow of Chester Russell. Born at Macon, Ga. July 5th.-1829. died at Macon, July 12th.-1891.

CHILDREN OF JOSEPH M. and CAROLINE A. BOARDMAN

1. Arthur Edwin, born at Macon, Ga., March 20.-1850.
2. Maria Theresa, born at Medford, Mass. August 1st.-1851. died at Macon, Ga., November 18th.-1854.
3. Juliet Morgan, born at Macon, Ga., August 20th.-1852.3. *(died at Mac May 5.-19*
4. Millie Pierpont, born at Macon, Ga., August 20th.-1852.3. died at Macon, Ga., November 28th.-1854.
5. Frederick Lord, born at Medford, Mass., June 4th.-1855., died at Macon, Ga., May 31st.-1856.
6. George Maynard, born at Medford, Mass., June 4th.-1855., died at Macon, Ga., July 6th.-1856.
7. Henry Horton, born at Macon, Ga., November 10th.-1856., died at Macon, Ga., December 24th.-1861.
8. Mary Elizabeth, born at Macon, Ga., March 1st.-1860., died at Macon, Ga., January 5.-1864.
9. John Lewis, born at Macon, Ga., March 29.-1863., died in Savannah, Ga., March 15.-1905., buried in Rose Hill cemetery, Macon, Ga.
10. Elodia Russell, born at Macon, Ga., February 23.-1866., died at Atlanta, Ga., October 21.-1905., and is buried there.

XII. ARTHUR EDWIN BOARDMAN, born at Macon, Ga., March 20.-1850. Baptized at Medford, Mass., by his grandfather, Rev. John Pierpont, September 14.-1851. Married in Brooklyn, N. Y., by Rev. Albert J. Lyman, October 20.-1875., to Reba. Warner Tallman, daughter of George Clinton Tallman and Julia Willcox, his wife. She was born at Utica, N. Y., October 15.-1852., died at Florence, Italy, November 21.-1923., s. p., and is buried there in the Laurel Cemetery.

9. JOHN LEWIS BOARDMAN, born at Macon, Ga., March 29.-1863., died at Savannah, Ga., March 15.-1905., married at Atlanta, Ga., October 6.-1891. to Mary Ellen Spence,

daughter of Nathaniel Cleland *Spence and his first wife,
Elizabeth Stevenson. Mary Ellen was born at Atlanta,
Ga., 1872., died at Wilmington, N. C., January 27.-1925.,
and is buried in Riverside Cemetery, Macon, Ga. Their
only child,

JULIET PIERPONT, born at Macon, Ga., July 4.-1895.,
married in Christ Episcopal Church, Macon, Ga., June 7.-
1922., to James Mason Mackenzie, of Charleston, S. C.
He was the son of John Leslie Mackenzie, born September
28.-1858., died 1898., and his wife, Ann Ennylin, born
March,-1859. James Mason Mackenzie was born at
Charleston, S. C., December 21.-1891. They had,

Mason Boardman Mackenzie, born at Charleston, S. C.,
August 7.-1924. Christened in Christ Episcopal Church,
Macon, Ga., February 1.-1925.

Juliet Nell, born in Charleston, S. C., December 27.-1926.
Christened at Grace Episcopal Church, Charleston, March
20.-1927.

*Folio 40 Appendix.

POWELL.

(B) JULIET MORGAN (Boardman.) married in Macon, Ga.,
Christ Episcopal Church, October 6th.-1874., to Harney
Twiggs Powell, son of Hugh T. Powell and Martha J. A.
A. Cottrell, his wife; born at Macon, Ga., August 14th.-
1847., died at Johns Hopkins Hospital, Baltimore, Md.,
June 9th.-1923, buried in Rose Hill Cemetery, Macon, Ga.
Their children are
(a) Miriam, born at Macon, Ga., July 18th.-1877.
(b) Justin Boardman Powell, born at Macon, Ga., April 20.-
1880.
(c) Hilda Augusta, born at Macon, Ga., October 14th.-1881.,
died September 29th.-1883.
(d) Mary Pierpont, born at Macon, Ga., December 31st.-
1885.
(e) Donald Winchester Powell, born at Macon, Ga., September 24th.-1889.

MIRIAM (Powell), (a), married in Christ Church, Macon, Ga.,
April 5th.-1899., to Lieut. William Yates, 1st U. S. Cav-
alry, Class of 1893. U. S. Military Academy. Son of
Andrew Yates and Josephine Roper, his wife, born at
Legareville, John's Island, S. C., September 27th.-1870.
Captain Yates was killed at Boise, Idaho, in an effort to
save one of his men, July 18th.-1906. Their children are,
William Roper Yates, born at Fort D. A. Russell, Chey-
enne, Wyoming, May 20.-1902, died at Laramie, Wyo-
ming, September 13th.-1903.
Harney Powell Yates, born at Laramie, Wy., December
25th.-1904.

MIRIAM P. YATES, on April 29th.-1919. married in Christ
Church, Macon, Ga., Rt. Rev. Albion Williamson Knight,
D. D., son of George Augustine Knight and Martha Demere, his wife, born at White Springs, Florida, August
24th.-1859.

JUSTIN BOARDMAN POWELL, (b), married at Centerville,
Md., October 30th.-1920. to Susan B. Mitchel, daughter of
James Archibald Mitchel and Eleanor Lux McKenney, his
wife, born March 13th.-1882. Their children are

Eleanor McKenney, born at Macon, Ga., May 30th.-1922.

Juliet Boardman, born at Macon, Ga., March 3d.-1924.

MARY PIERPONT, (Powell), (d), married at Macon, Ga., October 1st.-1907. to George Samuel Riley, Jr., son of George Samuel Riley and Eula Hatcher Hughs, his wife, born at Macon, Ga., August 19th.-1886., died there April 19th.-1918., and is buried in Riverside Cemetery. Their children are

George Pierpont Riley, (better known as George S. Riley, 3d.), born at Macon, Ga., July 26th.-1908.

Juliet Boardman, born at Macon, Ga., October 17th.-1910.

DONALD WINCHESTER POWELL, (e), married at Macon, Ga., November 22nd.-1913. Metta Cubbedge, daughter of Clarence Cubbedge and Henrietta Meyers, his wife, born at Macon, Ga., November 22.-1891. Their child

Miriam, born at Macon, Ga., January 29th.-1916.

(10.) ELODIA RUSSELL BOARDMAN, born at Macon, Ga., February 23.-1866., died in Atlanta, Ga., October 21.-1905. She was married in Christ Episcopal Church, Macon, Ga., October 23.-1888., to William Roland Chandler Smith, of Atlanta, Ga., born April 9.-1863., died March 29.-1902. He was the son of John Alexander Smith, born September 23.-1837., died December 29.-1920., who married, on July 18.-1860., Kate Gray Taylor, who died December 18.-1866. The only child of William Roland Chandler Smith and Elodia Russell Boardman, his wife, was

MAYNARD BOARDMAN SMITH, born at Atlanta, Ga., December 10.-1891. He married, for his first wife, in St. Luke's Methodist Church, Columbus, Ga., on April 24.-1913., Alice Lucile Brannon, second daughter of George Thomas Brannon, born August 27.-1857., died February 11.-1897., and Martha Stephen Green, his wife, born February 16.-1861. Alice was born, August 25.-1893, and died at Macon, Ga., December 5.-1918., and is buried at Riverside Cemetery. Their children are

(a) William Chandler, born March 19.-1914.

(b) Maynard Boardman, Jr., born May 30.-1916.

For his second wife he married, on February 14.-1920., Nell Putnam, third daughter of Joseph Albert Putnam, born October 19.-1868., and Amanda Seymore Tucker, born August 24.-1869. They were married December 19.-1889., and Nell was born March 29.-1900.

Maynard Boardman Smith, by his second wife had,

(c) Roland Pierpont, born January 8.-1922.

(d) Nell Elodia, born February 15.-1924.

Nell Putnam's grandparents, on the mother's side, were Richard Hillman Seymore, born 1844., died 1903. and Mollie Tucker, born August 15.-1842., died December 8.-1889.

APPENDIX

(*) Nathaniel Cleland Spence, born in Stirling Castle, Scotland, in 1843., emigrated to London, Canada, when twelve years old. Came South for his health and settled in Atlanta, Ga. He married for his first wife Elizabeth Stephenson in 1871. She was daughter of John Stephenson of Londen, Canada, and died in 1872., after the birth of her daughter Mary Ellen Spence.

(†) Captain OFFIN BOARDMAN, Commissioned December 11.-1775, Commander of the privateer Washington.

On January 15.-1776. the brig "Sukey", of 90. tons, laden with provisions, coal, &c., was brought into Newburyport by the "Washington", and the same day the ship "Friends", of 200. tons, was captured by a crew of 17. men in three whale-boats, under command of Captain Boardman. She was sighted in the offing, flying the English colors, uncertain what course to steer, having mistaken Ipswich Bay for Boston harbor. Led by Captain Boardman, and assisted by the outgoing tide, the three boats soon came within speaking distance of the ship. "Where are you from and where bound?," hailed Boardman. "From London and bound for Boston", came the prompt reply. "Want a pilot?", asked Captain Boardman. Receiving an affirmative reply, he offered to serve in that capacity, and was soon standing on the ship's quarter-deck, engaged in conversation with the English captain. Meanwhile the boat's crews, armed with boarding pikes and pistols, quietly ascended the ship's gangway and suddenly assumed a threatening attitude, whereupon Captain Boardman, taking command of the ship, ordered her colors to be struck. His orders were obeyed and a few hours later the ship was safely moored at one of the wharves in Newburyport.

(From the History of Newburyport, vol. 1., folios 614-15-16.)

POWELL LINEAGE.

Captain WILLIAM POWELL, born and married in Great Britain. (Wales probably.) Came to Jamestown, Va., in 1611. Killed by Indians, on the Chickahominy River,-1623. A subscriber to "The London Company." Member of first House of Burgesses,-1619. Commander at Jamestown, Commissioned Captain of Guards, belonging to Governor and Lieut. Governor. (For services of William Powell, see English Colonial Records of Va.)

JOHN POWELL, SR., youngest son of Capt. Wm. Powell, born in Great Britain-16-? Emigrated after 1623. Member of Virginia House of Burgesses 1632.

JOHN POWELL, JR., born 16-?, died January 12.-1718. Member of Virginia House of Burgesses, 1658,-1660,-1662,-1666.

GEORGE POWELL, third son of John Powell, Jr., died-1735.

LEWIS POWELL, SR., married Martha Sarah-?- (dates unknown.)

LEWIS POWELL, JR., born August 1.-1750., died after 1833. married Catherine-?- (Revolutionary Soldier.)

THOMPSON POWELL, born 1771., married Charlotte Hardy Bridges, died in-1844.

HUGH THOMPSON POWELL, born February 7.-1815., married October 8.-1835, Martha J. A. A. Cottrell, died January 3.-1859.

HARNEY TWIGGS POWELL, born August 14.-1847., married October 16.-1874, Juliet Morgan Boardman, died June 9.-1923.

MIRIAM POWELL, born July 18.-1877., married April 5.-1899, Lieut. William Yates, 1st. U. S. Cavalry. On July 18.-1906, Captain Yates was killed in an effort to save one of his men, at Boise, Idaho.

On April 29.-1919, Miriam Powell Yates married Rt. Rev. Albion Williamson Knight, D. D.

PIERPONT, - BOARDMAN, - POWELL.

Rev. JOHN PIERPONT, born April 6.-1785., married Mary Sheldon Lord September 23.-1810. died August 27.-1866. Their youngest daughter,

CAROLINE AUGUSTA PIERPONT, married, September 27.-1848. Joseph M. Boardman, born at Newburyport, Mass., May 10.-1808, died at Macon, Ga., June 28.-1893. Their daughter,

JULIET MORGAN BOARDMAN, born at Macon, Ga., August 20.-1852.? married Harney Twiggs Powell, October 6.-1874. He was the son of Hugh T. Powell and Martha J. A. A. Cottrell, his wife, and was born at Macon, Ga., August 14.-1847., died June 9.-1923. Their eldest daughter,

MIRIAM POWELL, born at Macon, Ga., July 18.-1877. married in Christ Church, Macon, April 5.-1899, Lieut. William Yates, 1st. U. S. Cavalry, class of-1893. U. S. Military Academy, son of Andrew Yates and Josephine Roper, his wife, born at Legareville, John's Island, S. C. September 27.-1870, Captain Yates was killed at Boise, Idaho, in an effort to save one of his men, on July 18.-1906. Their son, HARNEY POWELL YATES, born at Laramie, Wyoming, December 25.-1904. survives.

MIRIAM POWELL YATES, married in Christ Church, Macon, Ga., April 29.-1919. Rt Rev. Albion Williamson Knight, D. D., son of George Augustine Knight and Martha Demere, his wife, was born at White Springs, Fla., August 24.-1859.

INDEX

BOREMAN (Cont.)
Isabell 28 Jacob 33 Joan 28
Joanna 32 Job 30 John 28-30 33
Jone 29 Joseph 30 Margaret 30-
31 33 Martha 32-33 Mary 32 Mrs
Joseph 30 Mrs Margaret 32
Nicholas 29 Offin 33 Samuel 30
32 34 Sarah 30 33 Sarah Heard
33 Sisley 28 Thomas 28-33 30-31
William 26 28-30
BOREMAN-BOARDMAN, 32
BOREMAN-BORDMAN, 33
BOREMAN-BORMAN, 32-33
BORMAN, Daniel 32 Elizabeth 32
Hannah 32 Joanna 32 Martha 32
Mary 32 Thomas 32
BOURMAN, Thomas 32
BRANNON, Alice Lucile 39 George
Thomas 39 Martha Stephen 39
BRIDGES, Charlotte Hardy 41
BROUGHTON, Rebecca 22
BROWN, 29 Allice 29 Dorothy 15
John 15 Mary 15
BRUCE, Caroline Matilda 17
BURDEN, John 7 Margaret 7
BURGH, Hanysi de 25
BURGH, Herbert de Earl of Kent 25
John de 25 John de Baron de
Lanvallee 25 Robt de Earl of
Cornwall 25 Robt Earl of Moreton
25 Wm de (de Moreton) Earl of
Cornwall 25
BURGO, Harlamen de 25
BURGO, John de Earl Comyn Baron
Foulgues 25
BURNHAM, Margaret 33 Thomas
33
BURNS, Cynthia Mary 19 Mary
Ethel 19 Mary Lyman 19 Ruth
Evelyn Cavendish 19 Walter A G
19 Walter Hayes 19 Walt S M 19
BURR, Aaron 4
BUSH, J 13

CALHOUN, John C 4
CALKINS, Elizabeth 14
CAMPBELL, Archibald 10 Harriet
Louise 10
CARR, George 31
CARTER, Elizabeth 29 Felix 29
Margaret 29
CARY, Caroline Eames 23
CAVENDISH, Alice 27 Elizabeth 27
Frances 3 7 27 Margaret
Beauchamp 27 Thomas 27
William 27 Wm 7
CHAMBERLAIN, Anne 25 Richard
25
CHARLEMAGNE, 3 6
CHRISTIAN, Julia Tebeau 24
Phillip Jr 24
CLARIDGE, 29
COFFIN, Amos 33 Elizabeth 33
John 33 Sarah 33 Stephen 33
COLLINS, Anna 11 Anne 9 11 14
Charles 9 11 14 Elizabeth 3-4 9
11 14 16 27 John 11 Lois 11
Rhoda 11 Timothy 14
CONVERSE, Louise 20
COTTRELL, Martha J A A 37 41-42
COWEE, Abagail Merriam 9 Abigail
Merriam 21 Farwell 9 21
Millicent 9 21
CROLL, Janet S 18
CROSBY, Huldah Robinson 16
Jaazaniah 16 James 16 James
Allen 16 Mary Lord 16 Susan
Lillian 16
CROUCH, Clara A 22-23
CUBBEDGE, Clarence 38 Henrietta
38 Metta 38
CURSON, Catherine 25 John 25
DEMERE, Martha 37 42
DIGBY, Anne 25 Catherine 25
Elizabeth 12 25 Everard 25 John
25 Rose 25 Simon 25 Wm 25

DUFFILL, Cicero Franklin 24
  Myrtle 24 Rose Ella 24
EDWARD VI, King of England 7
EDWARDS, Jonathan 16 24
  Jonathon 3 Sarah 3 24
ELY, Elizabeth 14 Jane 14 Samuel
  14
EMPSON, Joan 7 Richard 7
ENNYLIN, Ann 36
ETHELINDA, Alfred The Great 25
FARLEY, Rev Dr 10
FARWELL, Robert 23
FELLOWS, Isaac 32 Joanna 32
FITSWILLIAMS, Mary 7 William 7
FITZ GOEFFREY, Isabel 26 John
  Fitz Piers 26
FITZ JOHN, John 26 Maud 26
FLANDERS, David 9 Mary
  Elizabeth 9
FOWLER, George W 10 Harriet
  Louise 10
FRANK, Frances 7 Wm 7
GARDNER, Henry B 18 Sarah
  Morgan 18 Sarah Spencer Jr 18
GOLDTHWAITE, Charlotte 34
GREEN, Martha Stephen 39
GREGORY, Dorothy 28
GRESLIV, Joan de 25
GRESLIV, Robert de Baron de
  Gresliv 25
GREW, Jane Norton 20
GREY, Anne 25 Reginald 25
GRIFFIN, Anne 25 Catherine 25
  Elizabeth 25 Nicholas 25 Richard
  25 Thomas 25
GUNDREDA, William the
  Conqueror 26
HAMILTON, Alexander 20 David
  Blair 21 Elizabeth S 21 Helen
  Morgan 20-21 Ian Morgan 21
  Juliet Pierpont 20 Laurens M 20-
  21 Marie Louise 21 Philip
  Schuyler 21

HAMILTON (Cont.)
  Pierpont Morgan 20-21 William
  Pierpont 20
HANSEN, Dorothy 22 Hulda 23
HARCOURT, Barbara 19 Doris M T
  19 Lewis 19 Mary Ethel 19 Olivia
  Vernon 19 William Edward 19
HARDWICKE, Elizabeth 27 John
  27
HARPUR, John 8
HARRIS, Elizabeth 8
HAVEN, Anne 9 Franklin 9
HAYNES, Edward 29 Jone 29
HEARD, Sarah 33
HEING, John de 7 Sarah de 7
HENRY II, King of England 25
HENRY III, King of England 25
HENRY VI, King of England 27
HENRY VIII, King of England 27-28
HOOKER, Mary 8 15 27 Samuel 8
  15 24 Thomas 15
HORTON, Sarah 34
HUGHS, Eula Hatcher 38
HUNTINGDON, Anne 9 11 14
HUTCHINSON, Alice 32 Hannah
  32 Richard 32
HYDE, Elizabeth 11 14 Jand 14
  Samuel 14 Samuel Jr 14
INGALLS, Francis Abbott Jr 19
  Mabel M 19
JAMES, Antoinette 23 Caroline
  Eames 23 Garth Wilkinson 23
  Joseph Cary 23
JENKINSON, Barbara 19 Julian C
  L 19 Robert Charles I 19
JOHN, Baron de Burgh 25
KATO, Yuki 18
KINGSTON, Duke of 8
KINGSTON, Earl of 3 8
KINSMAN, Mary 32 Robert Jr 32
KNIGHT, Albion Williamson 37 41-
  42 George Augustine 37 42
  Martha 37 42 Miriam P 37

KNIGHT (Cont.)
 Miriam Powell 41-42
LAFAYETTE, 4
LANCASTIRE, Elizabeth of 27
LANGLEY, Sarah 33
LANKFORD, Helen 7 Nicholas 7
LANVALLEE', Harvise de 25
LANVALLEE', Wm Baron de 25
LASALLE, Frances 11
LATIMER, Baron de Braybrooke 25
LATIMER, Catherine de 25
 Elizabeth 25 W de 25
LEE, Jane 14
LINCOLN, Abraham 5
LINGAN, Gen 4
LORD, Dorothy 12 Elizabeth 12-14
 26 Jane 14 Joseph 4 Joseph
 Lynde 34 Lois 14 Lynde 11 13-14
 26 Lynde Esq 9 Lynde Jr 14 26
 Maria Theresa 34 Mary 9 14
 Mary Sheldon 4 9 13-14 26 42
 Mary Wheldon 35 May Sheldon
 27 Richard 12-14 26 Thomas 12
 William 12
LOW, Deacon Thomas 32 Martha 32
LYMAN, Albert J 35 Mary 9 13-14 26
LYNDE, Elizabeth 12-13 25-26
 Elizabeth Digby 12 Enoch 12 25
 Hannah 12 26 Mary 13 26
 Nathaniel 12-13 26 Simon 12 26
 Susannah 12-13 26
MACK, Florence Stanley 17
 Madeline Doris 17 Wm Henry 17
MACKENZIE, Ann 36 James Mason
 36 Juliet 36 Juliet Nell 36 Mason
 Boardman 36
MACKINZIE, John Leslie 36
MANVERS, Annora de 6 Michael de 6
MANVERS, Earl of 7
MARSH, Ana 23
MASON, Joan 28 John 28
MATHER, Cotton 3 16
MCCOOK, Caroline A 19

MCGLENEN, Alice Irene 17
 Caroline Matilda 17 Edward
 Webster 17 Edward Webster Jr 17
 Henry Allen 17 Henry Aloysius
 17 Madeline Doris 17 Mary 17
MCGREGOR, Ellen Ryan 23
MCKENNEY, Eleanor Lux 37
MELTON, John 7 Thomasine 7
MEYERS, Henrietta 38
MITCHEL, Eleanor Lux 37 James
 Archibald 37 Susan B 37
MONTBONCHER, George 7 Joan 7
MOODY, Rebecca 33
MORGAN, Alexander Perry 18
 Alexander Perry Jr 18 Amelia 18
 Anne 20 Anne Tracy 18 Caroline
 A 19 Caroline Lucy 18 Catherine
 20 Charles Francis 20 Eleanor M
 19 Frances Louisa 18 Frances
 Tracy 20 George Denison 18
 George Hale 18 Henry S Jr 20
 Henry Sturgis 20 Jane Norton 20
 Janet S 18 John B 19 John
 Junius 19 John Pierpont 17-18
 John Pierpont Ii 20 John Pierpont
 Jr 20 John Pierpont Morgan II 18
 Josephine A 18 Juliet 9 17 Juliet
 Pierpont 17-20 Junius Spencer 9
 17-18 Junius Spencer Jr 17 20
 Louisa Pierpont 18-19 Louise 20
 Louise Converse Jr 20 Lucretia
 Perry 18 Margaret Croll 18 Mary
 Lyman 17-18 Sarah Spencer 17-
 18 Sarah Spencer Jr 18 Ursula J
 19 Yuki 18
MORTIMORE, Catherine 26
MULHOLLAND, Godfrey John M L
 19 Mary Norah 19 Olivia Vernon 19
NEAL, John 4
NEWARK, Viscount 7
NEWDIGATE, Hannah 12
NEWGATE, Hannah 26 John 26

NICHOLS, George 20 George Jr 20
Henrietta Mary 20 Jane Norton
20 Jane Norton Jr 20
NORTHHAMPTON, Lord 25
NOYES, Moses 24
PEARSON, Elizabeth 33 John 33
PENNOYER, Frances T 20 Frances
Tracy 20 Jessie Morgan 20
Katherine E 20 Paul G Jr 20 Paul
Geddes 20 Robert Morgan 20
Virginia M 20
PERKINS, Elizabeth 32 Jacob 32
John 31
PERRY, Josephine A 18
PERWICH, Rose 25
PIEFPONT, James 24
PIERPONT, Ana 23 Andrew
Warren 23 Anna 3 16 27 Anne 8-9
Anne Haven 9 Antoinette 23
Caroline Augusta 10 42 34-35
Clara A 22-23 David Cowee 23
David Jr 23 Eliza Jane 10 21
Elizabeth 3-4 9 11 14 16 27
Elizabeth of Lancastire 27 Ellen
Ryan 23 Evelyn 11 Florence
Frances 23 Frances 11 27 Frances
Tracy 23 Harriet Louise 10 Henry
27 James 3 8 11 14-15 21-23 26-
27 James 3rd 9 16 James Jr 8-9
16 21 James Lord 9-10 21 Joanna
9 Joanna Le Barron 21 John 3-4
8-11 14 16-17 21 23 26-27 35 42
John Jr 9 Julia Tebeau 24 Juliet
9 17 Juriah Harris 22-23 Lilian
24 Lilian Purse 21 Lois 11 Lucile
23 Margaret 27 Margery 23
Maria Cecelia 9 Mary 8 17 27
Mary Augusta 21 Mary Elizabeth
9 Mary Lord 16 Mary Sheldon 4 9
13-14 26 35 42 May Sheldon 27
Maynard Boardman 22-23
Millicent 9 21 Myrtle 24 Rhode 11
Robert 11 Robert Crouch 23-24

PIERPONT (Cont.)
Samuel 8 24 Sarah 3 16 24 Sweet
Mary Hooker 24 Thankful 3 8 16
27 Thomas Purse 22 William
Alston 9 16 William Marsh 23
Wm 27
PIERPORT, John 13
PIERREPONT, Anne 8 Anne de 8
Annora de 6 Baron 7 Edmund de
7 Elizabeth 8 Elizabeth de 8
Evelyn de 8 Frances 3 Frances de
7 Francis de 7 George de 7
Gervase de 8 Godfrey de 6 Helen
de 7 Henry 3 Henry de 6-7
Herbert 7 Hugh de 3 6 Hurst 6
Ingolbrand de 6 James 8 Joan de
7 John 8 Margaret 8 Margaret de
7 Martha 8 Mary 8 Mary de 7
Robert 3 8 Robert de 6-8 Sarah de
7 Simon de 6 Thomasine de 7
William 8 William de 6-8
Winifred de 7
POLEY, Allice 29 Elizabeth 29
Walter 29
POWELL, Catherine ? 41 Charlotte
Hardy 41 Donald Winchester 37-
38 Eleanor Mckenney 38 George
41 Harney Twiggs 37 41-42
Hildda Augusta 37 Hugh T 37 42
Hugh Thompson 41 John Jr 41
John Sr 41 Julieet Boardman 38
Juliet 37 Juliet Morgan 41-42
Justin Boardman 37 Lewis Jr 41
Lewis Sr 41 Martha J A A 37 41-
42 Mary Pierpont 37-38 Metta 38
Miriam 37-38 41-42 Susan B 37
Thompson 41 William 41
PURSE, Eliza Jane 10 21
PUTNAM, Amanda Seymore 39
Joseph Albert 39 Nell 39
RIDGEWAY, Maria Cecelia 9
RILEY, Eula Hatcher 38 George
Pierpont 38 George S 3rd 38

www.ingramcontent.com/pod-product-compliance
Lightning Source LLC
Chambersburg PA
CBHW060635280326
41933CB00012B/2042